Mia Levitin is a cultural and literary critic. Her ...
regularly in publications including the *Financial Times*, *The Spectator* and the *Guardian*. She is a graduate of the Wharton School of the University of Pennsylvania and previously had a career in mergers and acquisitions.

THE FUTURE OF SEDUCTION

Mia Levitin

unbound

First published in 2020

Unbound
Level 1, Devonshire House, One Mayfair Place, London W1J 8AJ
www.unbound.com

With the kind permission of Tortoise Media

Text design by Ellipsis, Glasgow

A CIP record for this book is available from the British Library

ISBN 978-1-80018-022-2 (paperback)
ISBN 978-1-80018-023-9 (ebook)

Printed in Great Britain by CPI Group (UK)

1 3 5 7 9 8 6 4 2

To Max

& your future seductions

FOREWORD

Where and who do we want to be?

How might we get there?

What might happen if we stay on our current course?

This is one of the five books that, together, comprise the first set of FUTURES essays. Each short book in the set presents a beautifully written, original future vision by an accomplished writer and subject expert. Read individually, we hope these essays will inform, entertain and challenge. Together, we hope they will inspire readers to imagine what might lie ahead, to figure out how they might like the future to look, and think about how, collectively, we might make the transition from here to there, from now to then.

Over the life of the series we aim to publish a diverse range of voices, covering as broad a view of the future as possible. We ask our authors to write in a spirit of pragmatic hope, and with a commitment to map out potential future landscapes, highlighting both beauties and dangers. We are hugely proud of each of the essays individually, and of the set overall. We hope you get as much out of reading – and arguing with – them as we have from the process of getting them out into the world.

This first set of FUTURES would have been impossible to publish without the enthusiastic support of Tortoise Media, Unbound and the subscribers whose names you'll find listed at the back of each essay. Michael Kowalski, Tortoise's Head of Product, introduced co-founder Katie Vanneck-Smith to the idea, and she made it happen. Annabel Shepherd-Barron's unparalleled strategic capabilities kept the project steady and on course. Matthew d'Ancona offered superb editorial guidance with extraordinary kindness and generosity of spirit, and Jon Hill's designs for the book jackets are elegant perfection. Fiona Lensvelt, DeAndra Lupu and their colleagues at Unbound have proved wonderfully creative and flexible throughout.

This first set of FUTURES essays was commissioned in autumn 2019, in the midst of the Brexit saga, and edited in spring 2020, in lockdown, as Covid-19 changed everything. As we write, it looks unlikely that, by the time you read this, our lives will have settled into any kind of normal – old or new. Still, argument, wit and enlightened thought remain amongst our greatest strengths as a species, and even during an era as stressful and disorienting as the one we are experiencing, imagination, hope and compassion can help us mine greater reserves of resilience than we might expect. We hope these essays can, in a small way, help us find some light at the end of the tunnel.

Professor Max Saunders, Series Editor

Dr Lisa Gee, Programme Director and Editor

May 2020

PROLOGUE

How much do our desires direct our futures? What invisible hand brings people together and how do they go from strangers to bedfellows? What do we – and what could we – expect of sex and intimacy?

When I re-entered the dating game after divorcing in my thirties, I expected my playbook to require a refresh. But the rules had become utterly unrecognisable during my time on the bench; it was, in fact, a whole new ball game. Courtship rituals de rigueur just a decade earlier – dinner on a first date, flowers, phone calls even – had come to seem as quaint as the quadrille, having made way for a murky morass of sexting, ghosting and 'hanging out'.

Hell-bent on cracking Cupid's new codes, I delved into the research. In my quest to comprehend WTF had happened and what the future might hold, I have grilled neuroscientists, evolutionary biologists and sexologists; dissected demographic data and Pornhub statistics; suffered through 111 first dates; and test-driven 'hug therapy' with a male underwear model (it's a tough job, but someone's gotta do it!). The dots have coalesced to form a picture of the landscape of love and lust revealing that unless we change course, we will be – in a word – screwed.

While I was enmeshed in my research, the #MeToo movement originally focused on sexual harassment and assault detonated into a broader discussion about bad dates and bad sex. Kristen Roupenian's short story 'Cat Person', which went viral after appearing in *The New Yorker*, depicted one such date in painful detail, exposing the pitfalls of modern courtship. Harassment is as old as the hills; coercion is in the very etymology of 'seduction', from the Latin roots *se* (away, apart) + *ducere* (to lead). But the consensus was that our new media were taking us backwards rather than forward, with porn warping sexual scripts and texting eroding the empathy needed to respect signals around consent. How, I wondered, could we go forward from here?

The tools we use to meet, mate and relate have evolved more in the past ten years than in the previous ten thousand, yet we arrive at them with a biology unchanged since the Stone Age. While technology may not spell the end of the species, it is naïve to think that wedging hard devices in the soft spaces between us is not fundamentally altering intimacy. As the media theorist Marshall McLuhan noted in the 1960s, we shape our tools but then our tools shape us, numbing the functionality they were designed to amplify. Today, it's our capacity to connect that risks being numbed by the very tools meant to enhance it. What's at stake – compassion, communion, desire itself – lies at the core of our humanity, and affects all of our futures.

THE FUTURE OF SEDUCTION

ARE WE HAVING FUN YET?

When I made my foray into the wild world of dating after my divorce, I set out to hack the game in the same way I had tackled other life goals, from getting fit to optimising productivity. Success in most endeavours held a linear, and quantifiable, relationship with effort: set a timer to write → up daily word count; endure HIIT workouts and egg-white omelettes → watch body fat dissolve. Simple, and with the outcome entirely in my hands.

Man-landing was, I figured, a numbers game. My back-of-the-cocktail-napkin calculation predicted that around fifty first dates should yield approximately five second dates, among which surely at least one would prove to be a good match.* And while I eventually hoped to find a partner with

---

* My ad hoc estimate was conservative: of approximately 30,000 first dates on OkCupid per night, co-founder Christian Rudder estimated that roughly 3,000 couples will end up in long-term relationships, a ratio which, applied to my target of fifty first dates, should have yielded five full flesh-and-blood companions.

whom to cosy up over the Sunday crossword, I was perfectly content to enjoy the company of Messieurs Wrong in the meantime. After the gut-wrenching process of trying to duct-tape a marriage together and watching it disintegrate anyway, fun seemed nothing short of necessary.

Wary of what I'd heard about the dick-pic-infested waters of digital dating, I started my hunt via more traditional routes. Bars, the mainstay of singles mingling, quickly proved a dead end in London, where the locals need to down vats of alcohol before gathering the courage to converse. At watering holes in my native New York, *Homo sapiens* are regularly observed approaching females of the species to strike up conversations. Englishmen, I learned, consider it rude to intrude. One does have the option of waiting until the requisite quantity of booze has been consumed to launch into rapid eyelash batting, but *caveat emptor*: if a man's speech is slurred, other fixtures are unlikely to be operating optimally.

'Go where the men are!' my friends chirped, trying to be helpful. I made exactly one excursion to the gym during 'man hours', sporting my most adorable athleisurewear and gym mascara, only to discover that grimacing through leg presses is precisely the last moment in which I wish to be chatted up (no matter how buff the chatterer). I considered forgoing my usual weekend activities of gong baths and moon meditations for more manly pursuits, like rock climbing. But faking a hobby that I would drop like a hot potato seemed to go beyond seduction to false advertising, like wearing a Victoria's Secret Bombshell push-up bra – which adds not one but *two* cup sizes. Pride prevented me from teetering around the aisles of Homebase in high heels looking helpless, as one book had suggested. And a remaining modicum of dignity kept me from heeding the advice of a Swedish friend – with whom I'd completed a yoga teacher-training course – to take up teaching yoga braless. ('My classes are *packed* with men!' she beamed.) Hot yoga indeed...

Eyes glued firmly on the prize, I dragged a friend to a silent speed-dating event, which advertised eye gazing as a fast track to intimacy. I had been intrigued by the potential power of sustained eye contact since reading the *New York Times* 'Modern Love' piece 'To Fall in Love With Anyone, Do This', in which Mandy Len Catron describes falling in love with a man after sharing the answers to increasingly intimate questions* followed by four minutes of eye gazing.[1] The catch is that Catron already *liked* the guy into whose eyes she dissolved into a 'state of wonder'. As our evening's MC shouted, 'Cross the room if you're wearing your favourite knickers!'

---

* Want to see a man beat Usain Bolt's sprinting record? Give the thirty-six questions a go on your next date. #7: 'Do you have a secret hunch about how you will die?' and #24: 'How do you feel about your relationship with your mother?' are real icebreakers. Ten bucks says you never make it to #25: 'We are both in this room feeling...' because there will no longer be a 'we' in the room.

during the warm-up games, all I wondered was whether my wing-woman would ever speak to me again.

A scheduling conflict made me miss the launch of pheromone parties, an LA export that never quite took off elsewhere. The idea is that you sleep in a T-shirt for three nights in a row, present said garment for sniffing by other singletons and note which of their tees tickle your nose buds. Pheromones have been proven to influence mate selection – in hammer-headed fruit bats at least, if not yet in humans. Prior experience of the olfactory offerings on the Underground, however, left me lacking enthusiasm for the pheromone party's obvious offshoot, Romancing the Armpit, in which – you guessed it – intrepid attendees skip the T-shirt conduit and put their noses directly into one another's exposed hollows. We were just one precarious step from real-life *Naked Attraction*.

If I was to drum up the necessary number of candidates to hit my target, digital dating began to seem unavoidable. Before I joined the masses on the apps, I warmed up with a brief stint on a legacy dating website. I was lured into signing up by the profile of a bearded self-proclaimed sapiosexual, who said he was looking for a special someone with whom to discuss Heidegger on his Harley. Once I had handed over my credit card details, he was nowhere to be found, leading me to suspect that the profile was fake. When I realised that

Mr Sapio had been chick-bait, I scrapped the paid subscription, took a deep breath and downloaded Tinder.

Really, I thought to myself, *how bad could it be…?*

LOVE ME TINDER, LOVE ME DO

While people continue to meet and pair off IRL – for life or for an evening – mating is increasingly mediated by a smartphone screen, with the delicate dance of seduction occurring primarily through the thumbs. Research out of Stanford showed that in 2017, 39 per cent of heterosexual couples and 65 per cent of same-sex couples in the US met online.[2] UK penetration is lower but rising: 13 per cent polled by YouGov in 2019 had met online; among 25- to 34-year-olds that figure was 21 per cent.[3] By 2040, eHarmony estimates that 70 per cent of couples in the UK will have met online.[4] What might that mean for the future of seduction?

'Swiping' apps – a digital version of hot or not – work by presenting a series of profiles of allegedly eligible bachelors and bachelorettes from a seemingly infinite deck.[*] Dig the

---

[*] It's a big deck for heterosexuals in cities. More on the paradox of choice later, but my perspective on seduction invariably reflects my own experience. I have included statistics on LGBTQ couples where available and I think the war wounds will be familiar to anyone in the arena.

card you're dealt, swipe right; not your cup of tea, swipe left. If both parties swipe right, you're connected to chat on the app's platform. When two people match, they can either send an in-app message or keep playing. Most of the time, users opt for the latter: one study found that fewer than 10 per cent of matches were consummated with even a half-assed 'hey'.[5]

Launched on a selection of highly social college campuses in 2012, Tinder spread like wildfire, boasting a billion swipes per day by 2014.[6] Not the brainchild of *Weird Science* geeks tinkering in a garage as one might imagine, the app was developed in Hatch Labs, an incubator within the media mogul Barry Diller's InterActiveCorp. Tinder was spun out of IAC in a public offering in 2015 as part of Match Group, 45 portfolio companies dedicated to increasing 'users' likelihood of finding a meaningful connection', including Match.com, OkCupid and Plenty of Fish.

Grindr, targeted at the gay community, had preceded Tinder with a location-based matching platform in 2009. Grindr tried developing a version for heterosexuals, called Blendr, but the app lacks Tinder's key paradigm-shifting feature: what's known as the 'double opt-in'. By allowing users to message only the people with whom they've matched rather than send unilateral hearts or winks, the double opt-in reduces the awkwardness of unreciprocated attraction and makes women feel safer. Unlike Blendr, users can't send photos on Tinder, reducing unsolicited nudes until both parties agree to migrate the conversation to WhatsApp, after which the cock shots and titty pics are free to fly.

By targeting a younger crowd, Tinder made swiping social and reduced the stigma of online dating. While dating sites were navigated at home alone with a fortifying glass of wine, Tinder was something to pull up and pass around the bar with friends. The app substantially lowered the barrier to entry: while setting up a profile on a traditional dating site often requires answering questions and paying a subscription fee, on Tinder – free except for premium services – all you do is pick a few photos from Facebook and you're off to the races.

A panoply of apps have proliferated on the back of Tinder's success. On Bumble – founded by Whitney Wolfe Herd, a co-founder of Tinder who sued the company for sexual harassment – the woman makes the first move, an experience which has made me much more sympathetic to lame opening lines.* Happn matches users geographically by showing profiles only of people whose paths you've crossed, making the Sunday-morning coffee run in your favourite tatty sweatpants a veritable obstacle course of dodging neighbours with whom you've had dodgy dates. Hinge, promoted as a relationship app 'designed to be deleted', differentiated itself by asking users to answer three ice-breakers to promote

---

* For same-sex matches, either party can start the chat.

conversation – although 'A shower thought I recently had...' may spark less depth than 'A social cause I care about...'

There really is something for everyone. The brilliantly branded 3nder – which had to change its name to the less exciting Feeld after a trademark infringement lawsuit by Tinder – offers to match you with people with similar interests, provided those interests involve group sex. Seeking-Arrangement matches Sugar Daddies and Mommas with aspiring Sugar Babies for 'mutually beneficial relationships'. Bristlr connects 'people with beards who like to have them stroked' with those 'who don't have beards, but would like to stroke them'. (I was an eager early adopter, only to beat a hasty retreat upon realising the fetish far exceeded my recreational lumbersexual proclivities, with many of the profile pics cropped to feature only facial hair.) Hater matches users based on their mutual *dislikes*: influencers, Trump, dating apps...

A MATCH MADE IN HELL

Despite the seeming sexual smorgasbord on offer, dating apps are surprisingly short on seduction. Longitudinal stud-ies show that singles are having less sex and fewer partners than a generation ago.[7] One study showed that half of Tinder users had not gone on a single date with a match made on the app. Even for casual sex, the stats aren't great: only 20 per cent of users reported having had one-night stands from the app, and the vast majority of those only once.[8] So much for the digital sexual revolution. If the 'sex recession' veers into a depression, the human race – let alone seduction – risks not having a future at all.

App aficionados, and the companies themselves, often liken matching on an app to catching someone's eye across a bar. Would that it were. For starters, there is no accounting for chemistry from a photo. (Luckily, we are not yet wiring up our underarms to scratch 'n' sniff profiles, but it's only a matter of time...) In one study of singles on the pull in a bar, researchers observed 109 distinct 'attraction tactics', including offering to buy someone a drink, sucking seductively on a straw, puffing out one's chest, and maintaining eye contact.[9] That's 109 signals that are not available to seduce on-screen, where straw-sucking is replaced by the significantly less sexy-sounding 'computer-mediated communication'.

Swiping turns us all into teenagers making snap judgments solely on the basis of looks. Women have long appropriated the male gaze. And since what the journalist Mark Simpson dubbed the 'spornosexual' physique – think Brad Pitt in *Fight Club* – became the straight male ideal, objectification has become an equal-opportunity endeavour. In a study of the most successful words for men to put on an online profile, 'physically fit' upped response rate by a whopping

96 per cent;[10] in another, the number-one word for men to use on a profile was – wait for it – '6ft'.[11]

Chemistry is key to compatibility, but looks turn out to matter far less than we think. In 2013, OkCupid launched an app called Crazy Blind Date, which sent about 10,000 people on blind dates with no information about the other person. In a result that flabbergasted the founders, the two participants' looks *had almost no effect* on whether they had a good time, even in cases in which one person was significantly more attractive.[12] In short, as Christian Rudder concludes in his book *Dataclysm*, people are preselecting on the basis of a criterion that makes no difference once they sit down on a date.

Because we're convinced that appearance is so important, however, the parade of hotness on our phones – whether on social media, porn or the apps themselves – can lead to disappointment with matches made. Research has shown that the initial impression of potential partners is adversely affected by recent or concurrent exposure to media showing highly attractive individuals.[13] Daters are aspirational online, with one study showing men messaging profiles that are 26 per cent more desirable and women 23 per cent more desirable, on average, with desirability calculated as a weighted measure of the number of messages received.[14] These are not just occasional acts of wishful thinking, concluded the researchers, but the norm. Not unlike income disparity, dating apps make those with the highest erotic capital very wealthy in choice. Choice, however, does not equate with happiness.

WHEN MORE IS LESS

One would think that an expanded pool of potential partners would optimise mate selection. In practice, however, while having too few choices creates feelings of despondency, having too many leads to decision paralysis. In *The Paradox of Choice*, the psychologist Barry Schwartz argues that infinite choice – whether of mutual funds, breakfast cereals or lovers – is exhausting to the human psyche and leads to greater dissatisfaction. When presented with too many choices, we are not only stunned, like a kid in the proverbial candy shop, but also less satisfied with the choice we eventually make, in what Schwartz calls the 'escalation of expectations'.

Researchers at the University of Wisconsin–Madison performed a study in which one hundred undergraduates were presented with either six or twenty-four potential matches and allowed to pick one. Those who selected from the larger pool were more likely to reverse their selections and were *still* less satisfied with their choice a week later than the group presented with fewer options.[15] An experiment run by the social psychologist Dan Gilbert at Harvard found that students told that their selection of a photo was irreversible – an arranged artistic marriage of sorts – were much happier with their choice than those who didn't have to commit.[16]

The average person in medieval times is thought to have laid eyes on fewer than 100 people in the course of a lifetime. An attractive young woman can rack up that many matches in minutes. Twenty years ago, while we may not have married a neighbour like our grandparents' generation, options were still finite: usually a handful of people met in the workplace, out and about, or introduced by friends. You did more to cultivate each option because you didn't know when the next one would come along. But with the whole world as a possibility, FOMO looms large.

The problem with the minimal-investment approach to seduction – bred by an overload of options on dating apps and infiltrating courtship more broadly – is that it is difficult to drum up desire in the absence of effort. This works both ways: we want to be wanted, and we treasure what we work for. Which do you value more: the one-hit wonders cycling through Spotify or the albums you saved up for, memorising the lyrics from the liner notes? We may think we prefer convenience, but effort can increase desire. In one study on speed dating, researchers found that when women changed seats instead of the men, they ended up liking more of the candidates than when they were the ones approached.[17]

For smaller pools, it's worth noting, a greater number of options does offer more utility. Although people identifying as LGB suffer from the same issues plaguing online dating (including harassment and racial bias), polls show higher satisfaction rates than heterosexuals,[18] and those with same-sex partners had more active sex lives.[19] Pew data showed that 55 percent of those who identified as LGB had dated online (twice the rate of heterosexuals), with about 20 percent having been in a committed relationship with someone they first met through these platforms.[20] Even before Grindr, the LGBTQ community had long been pioneers in mediated connections: there was an active queer culture in lonely hearts listings in the UK from the Edwardian era, and on Match.com from its outset in the 1990s.

To counteract cognitive overload for larger pools, the biological anthropologist Helen Fisher, who acts as a scientific advisor to Match.com, suggests stopping at nine matches. But there's no way to control the surplus of choice on the other side of the equation. The cost of the chance to swipe through and blow off options is that you, too, become an option to be swiped through and blown off. Some apps limit the number of matches in an attempt to increase user focus. Coffee Meets Bagel is one such app, popular with women, that offers its users only one 'curated' match per day. The bulk of daters, however, continue to opt for the apps that offer quantity – often finding swiping more arousing than meeting up, even for casual sex.[21] One study showed 44 per cent of millennials were on Tinder for ego-boosting procrastination – more than were looking for either hook-ups or relationships.[22]

THE EVOLVING MARKETPLACE OF HEARTS, HANDS & HOO-HAS

As the percentage of users skews male on most dating apps, at first glance it looks like young women hold the cards. But as the biological clock remains a reality despite advances in fertility treatments, the paradox of choice seems to be more detrimental to heterosexual women than men. The abundance of options available – even if imagined – may make men less inclined to treat any particular woman as a priority, explains the evolutionary psychologist David Buss. In communities around the world in which there is a surplus, or perceived surplus, of women, men pursue a mating strategy geared towards multiple casual relationships.[23] The continuing pull of the princess fantasy – from *Cinderella* to *Fifty Shades* – is less about being rescued than feeling unique. Being made to feel special – even if just for an evening – is at the crux of seduction regardless of gender.

Once upon a time, the feeling of scarcity could be manufactured by making oneself seem scarce. Playing hard to get to stoke desire is one of the oldest seduction tools in the box for both women and men. Xenophon's *Memorabilia*

THE FUTURE OF SEDUCTION

(*c.* 371 BC) has Socrates counselling the courtesan Theodote to make men 'hunger for her fare' by holding back until the men are 'keen as can be'. In Dorothy Parker's 1930 short story 'A Telephone Call', the heroine prays for the strength to resist calling the object of her affections. The 1995 *New York Times* bestseller *The Rules* instructed women to make themselves look busy. *The New Rules*, a 2013 update for the digital generation, even offered a handy cheat-sheet for age-appropriate text-back times. Set your iPhone timers, ladies!

As frustrating as the game can be, 'hard to get' does have a physiological basis, triggering the dopamine release associated with variable rewards. But in order for the strategy to work, someone needs to think of you as a reward rather than just a commodity. When users are sitting on hundreds of matches, applying 'the rules', even the updated ones, won't get you very far. Even if a woman has dutifully followed Rule #1: 'Be a Creature Unlike Any Other', the dearth of information on dating apps makes it nigh impossible to stand out from the crowd. Declining an invitation on Friday for Saturday won't increase intrigue; her suitor will simply move on to the next quasi-indistinguishable profile.

The dating handbook that characterised the aughts was *He's Just Not That Into You* (2004). Spawned from a popular *Sex and the City* episode and later adapted into a film, the book advised women to stop making excuses for men and move on until they'd found someone wooed by their wonderfulness.

Sage advice. It may, however, merit an update for the app universe. Hanging out is not dating, the authors warned. There is a word for a woman who maintains that standard today: celibate.

WILL YOU STILL LOVE ME TOMORROW?

The *New York Times* declared 'the end of courtship' in 2013, reporting that 'hanging out' had replaced dating. 'The word "date" should almost be stricken from the dictionary,' bemoaned a thirty-year-old woman interviewed for the article. 'It's one step below a date, and one step above a high-five.'[24] The rule of thumb used to be not to sleep with someone until the third date; now it's common practice to have sex *before* the first date, as self-revelation is considered more intimate than sex.[25] Uncommitted sex is nothing new; the shift is that the expectation is to be seduced *by* the sex act rather than *into* it. Far from free love, it comes at a cost. As certain scenes from the BBC1/HBO series *I May Destroy You* or HBO's *Girls* portray, sex embarked on with a shrug is rarely seductive.

Dating apps are not responsible for creating the hook-up culture, which sprang out of college campuses, but they certainly perpetuate it into adult life. Texting also plays a part: without instant forms of communication, hanging out looks more like dating because you have to make plans in advance. As participants are meant to play it cool, campus hook-ups often rely on blackout levels of drinking so that either party can disown what happened the next day. This is problematic for consent, not only because it makes memory fuzzy but because alcohol can cause men to overestimate sexual interest.[26] If we rely on substances to lower inhibitions, we don't get valuable practice in seduction, or sex for that matter, without that crutch. And shouldn't we be aspiring to sex good enough to remember the morning after? Perhaps this is why only a quarter of students are enthusiastic about the hook-up culture.[27]

Sadly, hook-up culture does not promote equal-opportunity enjoyment. According to research by the sociologists Elizabeth Armstrong, Paula England and Alison Fogarty, women only orgasm about a third as often as men do in first-time heterosexual hook-ups, and half as often as men do in ongoing hook-ups. The gap narrows substantially in longer-term relationships, in which there's more incentive to please your partner. Women are less likely to receive oral sex than men in a hook-up and less likely to receive the clitoral stimulation many need to climax than in a relationship, with a double standard at play as to who's entitled to pleasure in shorter-term arrangements.[28] Indeed, heterosexual women have fewer orgasms than any other demographic.[29] That's something I would like to see change – and I imagine I'm in good company. In another statistic that makes me want to weep big, hot tears, a YouGov survey showed that about a third of both men and women could not identify the clitoris on a diagram.[30] The new UK Relationships and Sex Education curriculum guidelines, updated for the first time in twenty years, are finally LGBT inclusive and include some teaching about consent. The word 'pleasure', however, remains absent.

The orgasm gap is exacerbated by pornography serving as sex ed. In the days of knights errant, pornography was instructional on giving women pleasure. Far from a how-to, today it's often filmed literally from the man's point of view. In the bulk of hetero content on the most-trafficked tube sites, the climax is male ejaculation, with the woman's pleasure primarily performative. Ever-ready, the women populating chat rooms, poolsides and dungeons do not require any seduction, writes Nichi Hodgson in *The Curious History of Dating*. This, she reckons, is not doing much for men's skills with the opposite sex. No wonder women feel they're getting the short end of the stick.

Although it turns out that the stick's not so happy either. Rates of erectile dysfunction have increased steadily since a glut of free porn videos became available, with up to a third of young men now experiencing ED.[31] Pornography has been around since cave paintings, of course, but the neurological effects of consistent exposure over high-speed internet access are a far cry from flipping through your father's *Playboy* collection. It may lead to 'arousal addiction', training the brain to prefer on-screen images to interacting with real-life sexual partners, creating a vicious cycle of performance anxiety. Experts are split as to whether porn is addictive, but rising rates of anal sex ('fifth base') among young people, for example, make it hard to argue that it's not affecting our scripts at all.[32] The easy option of porn removes a primal motivating factor for men to even bother to date: a male dating coach told me he counsels his clients to lay off of the stuff before an evening out so as not to squander valuable testosterone on a hunt for hentai.

What might we imagine for ourselves that's sexier and more satisfying? Dare we dream of a world that prioritises pleasure over performance? Incels ('involuntary celibates') claim men have a right to sex; how about women's right to pleasure? Unlike other advances for equality (universal child-care, say), bridging the orgasm gap would not cost a dime. Pleasure is not a zero-sum game: there could be more all around. What if a one-off sexual encounter inspired people to make more, rather than less, of an effort, because they wanted to make a good impression? What if 'locker-room talk' wasn't about grabbing anybody by anything but about how much pleasure you had given your partner? That would get my vote!

TINDERELLA AT THE BALL

Ready to take the plunge but out of my depth in the brave new world, I downloaded an e-course by a love-coach-to-the-stars to help me craft the perfect app profile. Under her tutelage, I selected pictures displaying my many facets: glamorous (showing cleavage), fun (drinking with friends) and down-to-earth (wearing 'no make-up' make-up and pretending to be engaged in a sport). Although high-angle selfies while flirting with the camera were said to fare the best, my 'smize'' communicated more *indigestion* than *come hither*, so I rolled the dice and went with a straight-angle smile. I even went as far as to wear red in my profile picture, a colour said to be like catnip to menfolk, in some subconscious shout-out to ovulatory facial flushing – or was it the bottoms of bonobos in oestrus? No matter. This girl was leaving nothing to chance.

I crafted the copy accompanying my profile to convey witty but approachable. Out went my professional pedigree and penchant for big books; MENSA Match, this was not. Out, too, went the word 'tactile', for fear of sending the wrong message. I ran my profile by a male friend, a veteran of online dating, who shook his head disapprovingly. 'Yoga,' he warned solemnly, 'is code for flexibility in bed.' The yoga stayed in. I was chagrined to see an eHarmony study identifying 'spiritual', 'articulate' and 'good listener' as among the worst words for women to use online.[33] Fortunately, my drinks

---

* Coined by Tyra Banks on *America's Next Top Model*, a 'smize' refers to smiling with the eyes, accomplished by slightly squinting while thinking of something delicious.

of choice – whisky neat and dirty martinis – were deemed 'hot' by the seductosphere, so if I slipped up and used big words or listened too well, at least it would be over a sexy drink.

Fretting over the text was, of course, a rookie error. With a googol of profiles to get through, 75 per cent of men say they swipe on the basis of only the first photo.[34] Aside from the required first name and age, men's profiles tend to share just their height (overstated, on average, by two inches)[35] and a job description, often something vague like 'director' (what or whom is being directed remaining undisclosed). Once in a while, they'll throw in a banal phrase along the lines of 'work hard, play hard'. Photos often show men holding babies, whom they proceed to rapidly disclaim in the accompanying text – a rather crude play on women's bio-logical urges – or puppies, just for the *awww* factor. Or, my personal favourite, snapshots of a lone sports car, with no man in sight.

The ladies are even less loquacious. Their profiles often include a quote falsely attributed to Marilyn Monroe (the Winston Churchill of Tinder) and breezy, generic interests: 'I love fitness and fun!' Hiking is disproportionately popular, although as the comedian Iliza Shlesinger explains it, a wom-an's definition of hiking is putting on the Lululemon yoga pants that make your butt look unreasonably good to stroll in the park with a friend and a latte. Pouty pics persist, often (troublingly) beneath false moustaches. Photos including *anybody's* baby are, of course, *verboten* for the *Fräulein*, with the vibe trying to relay: 'Hey, here I am having *such a good time* doused in festival paint. The absolute *last* thing I'm looking for is a relationship.'

The night my Tinder profile finally went live, I was as jittery as Steve Jobs before a product launch. Insecurities danced in my head like sugarplum fairies. To my relief, matches began dinging away instantaneously, a sound of validation that was not a little addictive. I would love to attribute my popularity to the effervescent charm bubbling through my profile or even the irresistible evolutionary pull of the red top, but it likely had more to do with the fact that men are three times more likely to swipe right than women, selecting, on average, about 46 per cent of profiles, versus 14 per cent selected by women.[36] As the behavioural economist Dan Ariely explains it, women tend to employ a 'budget' approach to dating, getting pickier the larger the pool gets, whereas men are more opportunistic, swiping right, basically, on anyone whom they'd fuck.[37] Provided, that is, they can be bothered to get off the couch.

A surprising number of people seemed to be on the apps just for the chat. A study out of Stanford showed that a staggering 80 per cent of single straight adults had not gone on a single date or hooked up in the previous year, leading the researcher to conclude that the main utility of the apps for heterosexuals might be 'for flirting or for browsing'.[38]

When did sex become a 'chore'? as one young man told a Vogue columnist when she tried to get to the bottom of the phenomenon of men flaking when it came time to meet up.[39]

Having weeded through the preponderance of pen pals, I finally had some dates lined up. Knowing that men are visual creatures, I enlisted a stylist friend to help me assemble the perfect first date outfit: a décolleté top in a soft fabric, skinny jeans (men apparently lacking the imagination to see through the baggier 'boyfriend' variety), dangly earrings (dudes dig those) and, critically, high heels and a red lip. If my efforts sound contrived or anti-feminist, rest assured that it was all rooted in the science. From the days when Cleopatra painted her pout with crushed bugs and beeswax, lipstick has been in the arsenal of women's war paint as a sign of fertility, as a full lip signals high levels of oestrogen. High heels not only add height, explains the anthropologist Helen Fisher, but by arching the back, tilting the buttocks and thrusting the chest out, they accentuate a woman's instinctive come-hither pose.

Uniform ready, from head to stilettoed toe, I brushed up on flirtation techniques in case my skills had gotten rusty. It is usually the woman who breaks the 'touch barrier' (or it was, pre-pandemic), indicating an invitation to come closer. The unmistakable signal of interest – as universal as the 'please bring the bill' gesture in restaurants – is a light brush of the arm. (In terms of signal strength, men rate a woman's rubbing her chest or pelvis against him second only to an explicit agreement to have sex, but I was unsure I could pull off the chest/pelvis rub at my local without risking arrest.) The love coach suggested subtly mirroring a man's body language, and even matching his breathing rate, to communicate interest. I learned that I should lean in – not in the Sheryl Sandberg way, but literally, with my body, to indicate that I was intrigued by what my date was saying. The good news? Flirting is like riding a bicycle: you really don't forget. The bad news? I rarely found myself wanting to lean in.

Over time, I tried most of the mainstream apps, as well as more selective ones with a vetting process like The League ('Harvard hotties'), Inner Circle ('the most attractive and inspiring singles') and Raya (the 'illuminati Tinder', popular with celebrities and wannabe celebrities). While they did cut time spent swiping by providing a smaller pool, the end result was much the same. The apps brought bodies – exquisite ones, even – but in the absence of seduction, my body just didn't respond.

The disappointment was not that I didn't emerge from 111 dates strolling through the flower market on Sundays with my better half. What was disappointing was the bleeding out of *eros* from the enterprise. More often than not, the dates bore more resemblance to job interviews than intimate *tête-à-têtes*. I wasn't suffering from nostalgia or struck with moral panic; it just wasn't very much fun. Surely we can do better for the future of seduction than this joyless present?

Ultimately, the best dating advice I received came not from a professional but from a friend who has long been a student of the womanly arts. 'Don't think of it as a search for Mr Right,' she suggested. 'Just consider it research about what you do and don't like.' Ladies and gentlemen, below is a short, non-exhaustive list of what dating apps have taught me I find utterly unseductive:

- A man whose very first message after matching contains any variant of 'Afternoon quickie?'/ 'Dom or sub?'
- Ditto for anyone boasting about the size of his member, with or without photographic corroboration
- Being asked to cough up £1.20 for an espresso on a first date (going Dutch on a bill involving coins is not egalitarian, people; it's just cheap)
- Anyone who cancels a date the day of, unless they are bleeding profusely, hospitalised or taking care of a family member who is bleeding profusely or hospitalised.

From what my straight male friends report, women are not behaving any better. If seduction is about attracting someone, are we really bringing our most magnetic selves to the party?

You are no doubt by now waving your arms frantically with a dating app success story. I am by no means contending that they never work, or that the relationships started on apps are any less authentic. One would hope that a kajillion matches per nanosecond would spark some magic, somewhere. I just suspect I would have had a better hit rate sitting on my stoop and intercepting the first hundred people who happened past. And I am not alone: as Pew's 2020 report on online dating reveals, 'By a wide margin, Americans who have used a dating site or app in the past year say the experience left them feeling more frustrated (45 per cent) than hopeful (28 per cent).'[40] Even those in the youngest age bracket – who have never known anything different and who include the demographic of most sought-after women* – report feeling that something is rotten in the state of seduction.

IT'S NOT YOU, IT'S MY IPHONE

Most successful seducers have the ability to make someone feel like the only person in the room, bathing the seductee in the light of their full attention. The only thing captivating our attention now, however, is a three-by-five-inch silicone

---

* I feel extremely fortunate not to have seen the chart showing that men of all ages are drawn first to the profiles of twenty-year-old women before embarking on my experiment. Ignorance is indeed bliss.

rectangle. Walk into a club packed with skimpily clad, delectable young ladies twerking to their hearts' content and where are the fellas looking? At their phones.

What is it about the smooth glass of a touchscreen that's become more seductive than stroking skin? Tech designers are adept at creating products that replicate our fantasy of an ideal relationship, the novelist Jonathan Franzen has observed.[41] The object gives everything instantly, asks for nothing and doesn't make a scene when it's replaced by a newer model. Our devices are sleek and sexy, and what they contain is designed to be seductive as well. Texting, searching and scrolling light up the same parts of the brain as gambling, viewing erotic imagery or snorting cocaine. Is it any wonder we have a hard time tearing ourselves away?

Smartphones serve as portals to elsewhere: subconscious reminders of all the other things we could be doing and people we could be with. In what the cyborg anthropologist Amber Case calls 'ambient intimacy', at any time, we can connect to anyone, anywhere. A splintering of the self across various media is impacting relationships across the board. But as our digital devices bed down in the boudoir, nowhere is the impact more sorely felt than in the sphere of seduction: among the suspected culprits of the sex recession are distractedness and increased entertainment options ('Netflix and chill' making way for just Netflix, if you will).

In addition to commandeering our attention, our devices lull us into a fantasy of a friction-free existence. Cocooned in a solipsistic world of our own design for three to four hours each day, engaging with the complexity of other human beings begins to feel effortful. 'A surprisingly large number of men say they're looking for "no drama" or something "drama-free" in their profiles,' reports Laura Hilgers in the *New York Times*.[42] It's as if high-maintenance has become any maintenance at all. Forty-seven per cent of millennial men used these terms in their OkCupid profiles (compared to 25 per cent and 12 per cent for Gen X and boomers, respectively). According to Tinder, heterosexual men are three times more likely to use such phrases than heterosexual women, while profiles of gay and lesbian users include the phrases much less often. Perhaps it's no coincidence then that early data on gay marriage suggests that the couples are happier, as they're better at negotiating their needs.[43]

A prerequisite for love is the overcoming of one's narcissism, wrote the social psychologist Erich Fromm in *The Art of Loving*. You will recall that Narcissus – numb to the affections of both male and female admirers – did not fall in love with himself but with his reflection. We long to connect but remain stuck, reaching for the unattainable object of our affection reflected in the black pool of the smartphone screen. It may smile and tilt its head coyly, but it can never love us back.

THE REAL DOPE

Could the ceaseless stimulation of the smartphone be hijacking the biochemistry of attraction that has been drawing us together since the origin of the species? One of the first questions in the standard diagnostic test for internet addiction is 'How often do you prefer the excitement of the internet to intimacy with your partner?' Morten Kringelbach, a neuroscientist and senior research fellow at Oxford, elucidated the biomechanics of pleasure over afternoon tea in a cosy room at the Queen's College known affectionately as the Queen's boudoir. Natural rewards, including orgasm, contain a built-in satiety at consummation relying, inter alia, on endogenous opioids. But when we're stuck in the dopaminergic excitement of seeking, Kringelbach explained, there is no signal telling us when to stop.

Compounding the problem when faced with an array of excitements is that dopamine is triggered by novelty. This evolutionary mechanism allows us to jump to action should a sabretooth saunter into Starbucks, but it's also what makes it tricky to stay focused on Tom when a notification of a match with Dick or Harry pops up. An acquaintance of mine was on a third date with a woman whom he actually liked (already a minor miracle), only to be caught on a dating app when she returned from the ladies' room. The dopamine hit was probably less powerful than the well-deserved whack she gave him with her handbag.

With a dopamine drip available 24/7, might we be less inclined to seek out sex? Twenty-nine per cent of Americans surveyed said they'd rather give up *all sexual interactions* for three months than downgrade to a 'dumb phone'.[44] Drugs that elevate levels of dopamine in the brain typically have a positive effect on the sex drive. But addictions are known to reduce interest in natural rewards. Sometimes cocaine makes users crave sex, Kringelbach told me, but often they just crave more cocaine.

The information we used to obtain in person about romantic interest – from eye contact, body language and tone of voice – must now be gleaned on-screen. Michelle McSweeney is a linguist who studies how intimacy is created over text messaging. The biggest predictor that a relationship is going to last? 'Specific questions that reference either a shared physical experience or a shared digital one,' she told me (i.e. paying attention and valuing time together). Another key indication of interest is text-back time. Long gone is the three-day call-back rule: hard to get plays out in minutes.

The Oxford anthropologist and evolutionary psychologist

Robin Dunbar believes that text messaging is nothing more than a quickening of the pace of the epistolary era: *billets-doux* were delivered multiple times per day in Victorian England. But with young adults sending 150 text messages daily (of only five words each, on average), we may be reaching the limits of what the nervous system can handle. Natasha Dow Schüll, a cultural anthropologist who has studied gambling addiction, compares the rollercoaster of texting with someone you like with the dopaminergic effects of playing slot machines. Leaving a message on an answering machine was more like buying a lottery ticket, she told me: you weren't expecting an immediate pay-off, and might even enjoy the anticipation.

A BASKET OF EGGPLANTS & PEACHES

Because it's asynchronous, texting is less intimate than calling, but it creates an illusion of closeness. As a mobile phone is carried on the body, messaging can feel 'symbiotic, like you're carrying the other person with you all day long', says John Suler, a psychology professor who specialises in online behaviour. Over text messaging, trust is created almost entirely through self-disclosure, rather than through a combination of factors, including eye contact and body language, when in person. Things can escalate more quickly online due to the lack of these visual cues, leading individuals to ask increasingly intimate questions. If an initial impression is positive, explains Joseph Walther, who has been studying the effects of computer mediated communication for nearly 30 years, then we tend to fill in the blanks with positives in an attempt to make the person three-dimensional.

There is also a documented disinhibition effect over digital communication. (Thus the ubiquity of nudes.) For some, the sense of anonymity and physical remove can impair judgment, not unlike the effects of alcohol. While sexting is used successfully by some couples to heat things up, it's a sorry substitute for sex itself. There are only so many permutations of passion that can be constructed with emojis, and over time, exchanges about who would like to put what where elicit about as much excitement as IKEA assembly instructions ('Insert peg A into hole B').

One study out of the University of Alberta of adults in committed relationships showed that 'hyper frequent' sexters (at least daily) reported a higher degree of conflict, feeling insecure in their relationships, and displayed lower levels of commitment and overall relationship satisfaction. Moderation in all things... According to the lead author, this may be because they were deprioritising other areas of the relationship. His research also found that the hyperfrequent sexters reported a high degree of 'technology interference' in their relationships – texting or emailing during face-to-face time with their partners and neglecting quality time together.[45]

If dull when dating, exchanging explicit photos or messages before ever having met someone can be downright dangerous. In 2016, the UK National Crime Agency reported a six-fold increase over a five-year period in reports of serious sexual assaults carried out by strangers met through online dating. The report highlighted that this was only 'the tip of the iceberg' as only a fraction of such crimes are reported. The vast majority of the perpetrators had no prior criminal record, leading the NCA to conclude that the spike was related to the growing use of dating apps.[46]

In many of the first-date sexual assault cases, the first face-to-face meeting took place within one week of having matched. Due to the escalation and disinhibition effects online, the semblance of closeness created can lead to the impression of being at a more advanced stage in the relationship. 'Exchanges of a sexual nature' had happened prior to more than half of the reported incidents. The NCA report concluded that perpetrators often had increased expectations of sexual activity at initial face-to-face meetings, and that they were then 'unwilling to accept that expectations differed'.[47] In 41 per cent of the cases, the date began at a residence.

One would hope that our signalling would adapt to new environments. But as the Zoom fatigue during lockdown attests, bodily evolution can't keep pace with technological advances. Will the future of seduction depend on technological innovation adapting to our bodies or going back to our bodily intelligence instead?

IS THERE A FUTURE
OF SEDUCTION?

As Clement Knox documents in *Strange Antics: A History of Seduction*, since the Enlightenment, there have been, by and large, two divergent seduction narratives – and never the twain shall meet. The first frames it as exploitation, in which deceit in pursuit of a sexual objective is often, although not always, carried out by men. The second narrative celebrates seduction as an emancipated pursuit of sexual pleasure. The conversation of late has been weighted almost exclusively towards the former.

Seduction as power play is nothing new. Samuel Richardson's *Pamela; or, Virtue Rewarded* (1740) is widely regarded as the first English novel. (It was certainly the first bestseller, a precursor to the publishing phenomenon of *Fifty Shades of Grey*, which was the best-selling book of last *decade*.) *Pamela* is the story of a fifteen-year-old girl from a recently impoverished family who is harassed by her employer, Mr B. His advances, which she systematically rebuts, crescendo from small gifts to groping to kidnapping. Inspired by Pamela's virtue, Mr B realises the error of his ways and asks for her hand in marriage. The dubiousness of her acceptance and a marriage across the class divide aside, the idea that a man had to work hard to pursue a woman influenced authors, including Jane Austen, whose work has informed our expectations of romance.

With no money, status or legal standing, and a pesky habit of fainting, Pamela was the epitome of vulnerability. All she had was her voice to refuse. 'What is left me but words?' she asks repeatedly. Women's voices, or lack thereof, have been at the heart of the conversation around #MeToo. Originally started by Tarana Burke over a decade earlier to help raise awareness of sexual violence, the hashtag took off in 2017 as allegations against Harvey Weinstein began to emerge and women took to Twitter to share their stories of sexual harassment and assault.

The backlash to #MeToo included some who voiced concern that it would kill seduction. Insistent or clumsy flirting is not a crime, said Catherine Deneuve; gallantry is not aggression. Male pursuit remains inextricably intertwined with our cultural expectations of courtship. Fewer than 1 per cent of heterosexual women who self-identified as feminists said they wanted to be the pursuer. Fifty-four per cent were happy to do a bit of both, leaving a full 45 per cent who preferred to be pursued.[48] In defending what she called a 'freedom to bother', however, Deneuve was conflating flirtation with harassment. Insistence in the face of resistance should be binned with catcalls. If we want any future of IRL seduction though, we should think twice about discouraging friendly approaches: a 2017 YouGov survey showed that 17 per cent of adults aged 18 to 29 believed that a man asking a woman out for a drink constitutes sexual harassment.[49]

What separates seduction from harassment is consent. For those not practised in affirmative consent – in which a clear, verbal 'yes' is required for every escalating step – the ability to read someone's cues to know if advances are welcome relies on a foundation of empathy. Frighteningly, empathy markers are falling, with one survey indicating a precipitous drop of 40 per cent among college students since the 1980s. Students surveyed were less likely to agree with statements like, 'I sometimes try to understand my friends better by imagining how things look from their perspective.'[50] Most of the drop in empathy has occurred within the past ten years, a trend that researchers link to the advent of digital communication. The good news is that the damage is reversible: after only five days gadget-free at a summer camp, children were better able to detect others' feelings in photographs.[51]

One hopes that part of the lasting legacy of #MeToo, which would bode well for the future of seduction, is that well-intentioned men will have learned when to back down. As recently as 2016, according to a study of 1200 college students and recent graduates, one third of women reported having had unwanted sex because someone was too persistent, and one out of four men still said women would need 'some convincing' to have sex.[52] We like to see things in black and white, categorising men who assault as monsters. In interviews with over a hundred young men for her book *Boys & Sex*, however, Peggy Orenstein found that even good guys can do bad things. It's not that young men can't read cues on consent, she concluded, but that they have been conditioned to prioritise their pleasure and interpret the cues through the lens of their own desires. Sex education, as such, should go beyond the basics of consent to show boys how this conditioning might be impacting their behaviour.[53]

Sadly, the word 'seduction' has been further sullied by the pickup artist community, who peddle their wares under the moniker and congregate on Reddit at r/seduction. Popularised by Neil Strauss's 2005 *New York Times* bestselling *The Game*, pickup 'artistry' teaches seduction techniques that prey on women's insecurities; among the instructions for aspiring lotharios is how to overcome 'last-minute resistance'. Seen in sanitised form in films like *Hitch* (2005) and *Crazy, Stupid, Love* (2011), the movement fell out of public favour when the incel Elliot Rodger's UC Santa Barbara 2014 killing spree showed the tragic potential of toxic masculinity. In 2015, Strauss published *The Truth*, a *mea culpa* describing his sex addiction – which *GQ* dismissed as 'complete and utter bollocks'.[54] Despite

Strauss's renunciation of the pickup techniques as 'objectifying and horrifying', *The Game* was reprinted in 2016 and he continues to receive royalties from its sales.

The Game advised men to think of picking up 'hotties' as a video game – a precursor to dating apps as gaming. On the more sinister spectrum of the manosphere, as Laura Bates writes in *Men Who Hate Women*, incels refer to women as 'foids', a shortening of 'female humanoid', in order to dehumanise them. When people imagine the future, they often worry about sexbots replacing women. But as plenty of options for ersatz intimacy exist already, as far as seduction goes, I worry more about people objectifying humans than personifying objects.

LOVE IN THE TIME OF CORONA

Until early 2020, the future of seduction looked reasonably predictable based on the present: a rather bleak onanistic landscape employing increasingly 'smart' devices. But as COVID-19 spread, any certainty about the future in any domain was rocked to the core.

As life went even more digital during lockdown, the inversion we had been heading towards for over a decade was nearly complete: many of us in the West had gone from a life engaged in the world interspersed with screen time to existing almost entirely online, with the outside world a place to dip into from time to time. Seduction took a strange twist, as physical intimacy became potentially perilous for the first time since the AIDS epidemic, leading singles to date fewer people at a time and have exclusivity conversations sooner.

Government guidelines on sex during lockdown varied by geography. The Dutch were counselled to limit themselves to one *seksbuddy*. Single Brits pored over the rules in search of a loophole (outdoor orgies? elite athletes?) until 'support bubbles' effectively lifted the sex ban. Officials in New York and LA began by preaching abstinence: 'You are your safest sex partner,' wrote the New York Department of Health, and the 'next safest partner' is someone in your household. The guidelines were later updated to acknowledge inter-household activity by recommending wearing face masks and avoiding kissing for safer sex. 'Make it a little kinky,' suggested their COVID-19 factsheet. 'Be creative with sexual positions and physical barriers, like walls, that allow sexual contact while preventing close face-to-face contact.'

For those not busy building state-sanctioned glory holes, dating app traffic soared during lockdown. Tinder had 3 billion swipes on 29 March alone, the highest number recorded in the app's history.[55] The daily average Swipes™ (yes, it's actually trademarked) of female users under 30 were up 37 per cent, which got Match Group excited. 'Female usage and engagement is a key driver for a dating product's success,' they told shareholders.[56] OkCupid also noted an uptick, with women sending 40 per cent more intro messages than previously.[57] Spend on premium services, however, went down with the economy.[58]

In light of rules around social distancing, the pandemic ushered in a new era of video dating. Bumble's in-app video chatting, a feature many users didn't even know existed, increased 93 per cent in the two weeks after Trump declared a national emergency.[59] Hinge also introduced a 'date from home' feature to indicate if matches were up for a video chat or phone call. Teams at both Tinder and Facebook Dating got busy adding video functionality to their platforms to accommodate the surge in interest. Feeld fielded remote threesomes, and queueing for The League's video speed-dating events began to rival the wait for an Ocado slot. By adding the dimensions of voice and mannerisms, video is one step closer to sussing out what it's like to be with someone. Provided the apps could screen for safety – i.e. it didn't devolve into Chatroulette – some users planned to continue using video as a way to screen dates before meeting face to face.

As physical borders contracted, the digital dating universe expanded: Bumble let people match with anyone in their country and Tinder offered its premium Passport function –

traditionally used by people to line up dates before a holiday – for free during lockdown. Airbnb and Bumble teamed up to curate virtual first dates in exotic locales, from a Turkish coffee-grind reading (hopefully predicting a wonderful future together) to 'Meet the Woolly Sheep of My New Zealand Farm'. Virtual Reality Looking For Partner (VRLFP) – 'a community for people interested in dating, hook-ups, friend-ship and/or roleplaying in virtual reality' – left the physical plane behind altogether. VR porn also saw increased traffic, offering experiences in places people missed: outdoors, abroad, in restaurants and, yes, hair salons.

Many commentators highlighted the positive aspects of distance-dating, praising the slow burn of delaying physical intimacy, deeper conversations around safety, and longing associated with separation. If one positive thing came out of lockdown with regards to seduction, people realised how much they missed human touch. Some singles complained of increased aggressivity, however, with a ramp-up in unsolic-ited nudes and pressure to break lockdown rules to meet up. Others wondered whether video chatting with people in far-flung locations, whom you had no chance of meeting anytime soon, was yet another way of avoiding intimacy. In its roundup of pandemic dating alternatives, *Time Out* London kept it real: 'None of them is as good as going to the pub for a couple of drinks and then going back to theirs.'[60]

IF YOU CAN'T BEAT 'EM, JOIN 'EM

Even before lockdown, dating apps were a booming business. Trading in insecurities, dating is one of few services in which dissatisfaction leads users to question themselves instead of the product, and even increase spending to up the odds of success. According to the analytics firm App Annie, dating app spend has doubled in the past two years, to $2.2 billion globally in 2019. Tinder is the highest-grossing non-gaming app: since 2015, it has seen an impressive 123 per cent compounded annual growth rate to over $1.2 billion revenue.[61] Although the parent company does not split out its portfolio companies in its reporting, options conversions in 2017 valued Tinder at $3 billion.[62]

Match Group's stock price dipped when Facebook announced its plan to enter the dating game in 2018 but quickly recovered. Despite the massive advantage of data on its 2.6 million active users, for now analysts don't consider Facebook Dating a threat to Tinder's business model. Match Group believes that there is still room for growth in North America and Europe, where more than half of singles have yet to try dating apps, and projects higher growth for markets in less-saturated geographies with mobile-savvy singles.[63]

While the dating market is fragmented at the tails – with smaller apps including those matching on religion or niche interests – Match Group holds a substantial chunk of the big players. While Tinder remains its crown jewel, it acquired OkCupid in 2011, Plenty of Fish in 2015 and Hinge in 2019. In an interesting twist in light of bad blood between the founders of Bumble and Tinder, Match courted Bumble for acquisition in 2017, reportedly making a low-ball offer of $450 million for its biggest competitor. Spurned as a suitor, Match sued Bumble for patent and trademark infringement. Bumble retaliated with its own lawsuit, saying that Match had pretended to be interested to gain access to confidential information and steal trade secrets. 'We swipe left on you,' read a Bumble ad addressed to Match. 'We'll never be yours. No matter the price tag, we'll never compromise our values... consider yourselves blocked.'

However the apps end up splitting the market between them, their popularity has made other matchmaking businesses more difficult to operate, reducing consumer choice. A matchmaker at a high-end agency told me that her clients, who were always exigent given the hefty fee of the service, come in with ever-longer laundry lists of must-haves and deal-breakers. The shutting down of Guardian Soulmates, a mainstay of dating in the UK since 2004, was a direct casualty of free apps. Not everyone was sad to see Soulmates go. 'Where now will I find perfectly nice people I don't fancy to have a drink with and then never see again?' the novelist Elizabeth Fremantle quipped on Twitter, taking the words right out of my mouth.[64] But some were more sentimental about Soulmates. In *The Spectator*, Zoe Strimpel, the author of *Seeking Love in Modern Britain*, called its demise 'an epic final nail in the coffin of the old era of courtship'.[65]

A consequence of an increasing reliance on dating apps is that people are becoming more hesitant, and unpractised, at unmediated seduction. The social anthropologist Jean Smith told me that some participants in a masterclass she taught on flirtation asked her to set up an online forum so they could 'wink' at those whom they had been too shy to approach during the cocktail hour. This, having just dedicated hours to developing that very skill! Despite the prevalence of apps, a full 84 per cent of millennials surveyed said they would still prefer to meet someone organically.[66] And yet they fear they are losing the aptitude to do so: a School of Life class I attended on the art of conversation was filled mostly with younger participants who felt unable to relay their text selves into real life. Northwestern University's class on intimacy is dubbed 'the most popular course on campus'. One of the assignments? Asking someone out on a date.[67]

As I learned on one of Smith's 'fearless flirtation' courses, striking up conversations IRL can be as simple as asking a question to establish rapport, e.g. 'Can you recommend a beer on tap?' The revelation is that if someone is interested in talking to you, your opening gambit *does not matter a lick*. If they're not interested (take heed PUAs!), you respectfully retreat. Provided you don't stake your self-worth on strangers, a smile is a low-cost investment: if it goes unreturned, what, really, have you lost? Flirtation doesn't even have to have sexual undertones or romantic intent; at its base, it is nothing more than cultivating a sense of playfulness and openness to the possibilities of conversation. (You might discover a new lager!) There are plenty of people out there in the wild, it turns out, if we just lift our heads (and our AirPods) long enough to notice.

BE STILL MY BEATING HEART

The rapid rise of dating apps signalled a loss of faith in the matching algorithms of dating sites, but if someone were able to isolate that elusive spark, it could still be a game changer. Bilateral preferences are much trickier to program than Netflix or Spotify making suggestions based on past choices, but unlike friends and family, which are a 'static' matching technology, there's at least a chance programmers could crack it.[68] Imagine all of your ex-lovers in a room: you might not be able to find a formula, but there are probably more common threads than just that you found them appealing after a couple of drinks. The challenge is two-fold: determining what those threads are and extracting that data from potential new partners.

Human beings are ill-equipped to know what we want, and less guided by reason than we'd like to believe. Answers based on traits and preferences have proven ineffective at determining compatibility, with even deal-breakers often not mattering once people meet. The social psychologist Eli Finkel, the director of the Relationships and Motivation Lab at Northwestern University, believes the future lies in using dyadic data, observing rather than predicting compatibility from an initial interaction. Non-conscious synchrony emerges when two people are interested in one another: within minutes, pupil dilation, sentence structure and laughter begin to synchronise. Reading these cues can indicate whether two people like each other and, Finkel's research has shown, is a predictor of long-term compatibility.

Given the growing popularity of video dating, daters might be open to having biometric measures such as pupil size or pulse measured during a video chat to save time and the agony of the guessing game of 'loves me' or 'loves me not'. But chemistry isn't always instantaneous: some matchmakers insist on a three-date minimum because attraction can develop over time. Harvesting biometric data also raises chilling privacy concerns, as it's information that could be misused to gauge and manipulate emotion. Biometric data could enable corporations and governments to not only predict affect but exploit it in order to sell us something – whether products or politicians.

Ethical issues also arise with using artificial intelligence (AI) for matching. Until it was booted from Tinder, which bans third-party apps, a service called Bernie used 'AI, deep learning and facial recognition' to automate swiping and chatting. The founder claimed an accuracy rate of 99.86 per cent among clients – although it may be more of an indication of the banality of app chat than Turing test-sophistication that users couldn't tell that Bernie was a bot.[69] Using AI presents other problems besides tricking people into thinking they're talking to a real person. While digital dating has had a noticeable positive impact in increasing interracial marriages, there is a persistent racial bias on dating apps, which could be exacerbated if encoded by algorithms basing themselves on previous selections. And if user preferences were shared with third parties, what's to stop advertisers from tailoring ads to use people with facial features they know you like?

Another creepy matching methodology involves genetic testing. For the price of a $249 DNA test, GenePartner claims to determine 'genetic compatibility', which, it says, 'results in an increased likelihood of forming an enduring and successful relationship, a more satisfying sex life and higher fertility rates'. The company offers itself as a complementary service to matchmakers and online dating sites, who are meant to do their part in sussing out a couple's 'social compatibility'. For GenePartner, chemistry is nothing more than 'the body's receptive and welcoming response when immune systems harmonise and fit well together', which can be measured.

The matching potential of the genome is not entirely without merit: kissing is hypothesised to be subconsciously used by women to gauge the health and genetic make-up of a potential mate through saliva, as well as for eliciting arousal through the exchange of hormones. But sharing DNA information with a platform rather than through a kiss raises risks that data can later be sold on to insurance companies or law enforcement agencies, or used in paternity disputes. Further, selecting for genetic traits can't help but carry a whiff of eugenics. George Church, a Harvard Medical School geneticist, has designed a dating app that compares DNA and screens out matches if they have similar genetic mutations that could result in hereditary diseases like Tay-Sachs. Church dismisses concerns about eugenics as clickbait, but fears of the potential misuses of genetic engineering in the wrong hands are tough to shake after sterilisation by the Nazis.

The cyberpsychologist Mary Aiken expects that the 'instamacy' of meeting in online environments will only accelerate with advances like DNA screening and virtual dating with full-sensory VR. As she writes in *The Cyber Effect*, the concern is that a future long on science risks being short on love. There is also something profoundly unsexy about reducing attraction to its chemical components. Do we not want to retain a hint of mystery and serendipity?

AN INVITATION TO DREAM...

I had hoped for a blueprint from the past that might inspire a vision for a brighter future for seduction, but truth be told, there was no halcyon era: our sexual relationships have always been at the mercy of gender norms and market dynamics. The couples forging forward with the most authenticity at present seem to be those who don't have the option of a beaten path to follow. One of the most beautifully rendered love (and sex) stories I have read is Maggie Nelson's *The Argonauts*, in which she recounts her relationship with the transgender artist Harry Dodge. Queer couples are also ahead of the heterosexual community in negotiating the terms of openly non-monogamous relationships, rather than falling into the hurtful hetero norm of adultery.[70]

We can all learn from addressing the desires of individuals rather than defaulting to traditional gender roles. As we saw earlier, same-sex couples have more orgasms than heterosexual women. Once two straight people agree to have sex, communication often shuts down. The columnist and podcaster Dan Savage suggests that everyone adopt the 'four magic words' that gay men use when getting intimate: *What are you into?*[71] Straight men are more likely to ask 'yes' or 'no' to a series of predefined options, reports Peggy Orenstein.[72] Not assuming that sex is a straight path to penetrative sex might also serve to increase appetite. One survey showed that 30 per cent of women report pain during vaginal sex and 72 percent report pain during anal sex, with many not telling their partners it hurts.[73] As reported by *The Week,* sex researchers say that by 'good sex', men often mean they had an orgasm, whereas women mean without pain.[74] That is a tragically low bar.

If you want to make women freer sexually, adds Savage, 'make the world safer for women'. While the vision that sexual equality would bring about equality elsewhere may be utopic, the inverse does have an impact: as long as women fear for their safety and reproductive consequences, they will bear the brunt of the risks associated with casual sex. Social consequences remain as well. Women are told to own their desires, but those desires can still be used against them, as we repeatedly see in rape trials. After the 2018 murder of British backpacker Grace Millane in New Zealand, her sexual history was brought up both in court and in media coverage of the trial.

The language of consent is a start, but it is insufficient to address all of the intricacies of sex. Consent is what makes sex legal, says Shafia Zaloom, a sex education specialist, but it doesn't guarantee that it's ethical. Ethical sex takes into consideration how your actions affect your partner and others. For sex to be *good* on top of legal and ethical, she adds, it should be pleasurable and mutually satisfying.[75] Imagine if the 519,000 members of r/seduction were trading sex tips rather than pickup strategies? Or that pornography went back to being instructional on female pleasure? The internet is difficult to police or legislate, but we can at least develop more awareness of what we're consuming and its effects on our expectations of sex. And support more ethical and, frankly, helpful porn.

For those of us with inherited heterosexual gender assumptions, we are products of programming that is not so easy to shake. Although 75 per cent of heterosexual men in a 2019 survey said they were happy with a woman messaging first on a dating app, only 19 per cent of women do.[76] Even on Bumble, in which the woman makes the first move, the man often takes the lead after the initial contact.[77] It may be challenging for those of us on whose brains the script is indelibly imprinted to change. If we want more choices for the future, however, we have to hold those producing popular culture to account for greater inclusivity and more agency among female characters.

Television and movies have a big impact on our subconscious expectations for relationships. It's thought, for example, that *Will & Grace* beaming gay characters into living rooms across the country contributed to growing acceptance of same-sex marriage in the US. While a generation tries to unravel the damage from Disney commodifying their princess franchise, I give credit to *Frozen 2* for being more forward-thinking than *Frozen* and join fans in rooting for Elsa to come out in *Frozen 3*. We also need more content from creators like Michaela Coel, whose trailblazing series *I May Destroy You* offers such a nuanced consideration of consent, including depicting 'stealthing' (removing a condom without consent midway) and several situations that are consensual but not necessarily ethical.

While sexuality has progressed in so many ways in the past half-century – with hard-won freedoms around marriage equality and gender identity – the sexual conversation for heterosexual women seems to have stalled. We are stuck with a polarity of predation on one side and a narrow version of sex positivity on the other. Far from the female empowerment envisioned during the sexual revolution, we have adopted a narrow and stereotypically male shorthand for sexiness. What if we were to reclaim the very definition of seduction from overcoming resistance to its other meaning of emancipated pleasure? What uncharted territory might we discover if we let the thread of desire lead us, rather than following a pre-programmed script? What would it feel like to lose the camera of self-consciousness clocking our every move?

Confidence that one's 'no' will be respected is a prerequisite of voicing an enthusiastic 'yes'. But with so much attention focused on bad sex, we should not lose sight of what good sex might look like, too. The majority of millennials say that sex is better if you love someone, yet we shy away from talking about the expansive possibilities of sex, let alone love.[78] The joy of sex – good sex – is that it can free us not only from thought but from what Emerson referred to as the jail of self-consciousness. The word 'ecstasy' comes from the Greek *ekstasis* – standing outside oneself. Sex is also one of few arenas for adults to play in. The biggest erogenous zone is the mind, with suggestion more arousing than exhibition, and anticipation a large part of excitement. By fast-forwarding through the foreplay of our own sex scenes with the goal of expedient ejaculation, we sell ourselves incredibly short. What if we were to drop the devices to re-engage in the fullness of sensory experience, alive to the power of embodied presence within ourselves and atuned to others'? Imagine that.

It may not be possible to exhume chivalry, but how about dusting off a measure of thoughtfulness all around? The pandemic has given us occasion to pause and consider how it is we want to live, at a moment when we have reached the apotheosis of individualism. We can rethink our approach to social care, healthcare and the environment or we can revert back to the old normal. We can engage in the world and the people who populate it, in all of their glorious messiness, or spend our one wild and precious life swiping them away. Choose your own adventure.

When I found myself behaving like the natives – ghosting, making snap judgments and unable to muster any measure of enthusiasm – I knew it was time to hang up my cleats.

Who wants to be the Beckham of Bumble? I'll be on my stoop nursing a whisky, talking to the humans who happen by. I learned the hard way that man-landing is not a numbers game. Connection can't be conjured, but we can cultivate the conditions that give it a chance to arise. I daydream less about Prince Charming swooping in than a society in which tenderness is celebrated rather than dismissed, and where desire isn't considered an embarrassment.

Eventually, either Big Tech will go the way of Big Tobacco or we will become transhuman ('Siri, please give me an orgasm...'). In the meantime, as we march towards the fourth industrial revolution – in which the physical, digital and biological worlds are predicted to merge – we would do well to safeguard the soft, animal underbelly of intimacy. The kids, I hope, will be alright. What do I wish for my son, as he teeters on the precipice of his own explorations of sexuality? I hope that when he gets into bed with someone, they have not lost the capacity for wonder. I hope he manages the conflicting signals around masculinity to continue to be a gentleman. I hope he loves and is loved, respects and is respected, and has a fuck-ton of (mutual) fun.

Most of all, I hope that when my son falls in love, he does so with his whole heart. We go to such great lengths to protect our children from getting hurt, and the cultural shift away from intimacy seems to be part of a broader retreat to safety. Our society is deeply uncomfortable with dependency and vulnerability, notes the psychotherapist Esther Perel. But both are necessary for good intimate sex.[79] Vulnerability takes practice, says Daniel Jones, the long-standing editor of the 'Modern Love' column; he worries that our tools are not allowing us to gain this valuable practice.[80]

When the world feels uncertain, vulnerability can feel frightening. We play it safe, expecting that someone will come along and jolt us out of our indifference. But to enjoy the connection we crave, we must make up our minds to risk something. Love, wrote Ovid in his *Ars Amatoria* – the first known seduction manual – is 'no assignment for cowards'. What are you ready to risk?

AFTERWORD

In 1924, inspired by a sensational essay they had published the previous year, the publishers Kegan Paul launched a series of small, elegant books called To-Day and To-Morrow. The founding essay was *Daedalus; or, Science and the Future*, and its author, the biologist J. B. S. Haldane, made several striking predictions: genetic modification, wind power, artificial food. But the idea that captured the imagination of his contemporaries was what he called 'ectogenesis' – the gestation of embryos in artificial wombs. Haldane's friend Aldous Huxley included it in his novel *Brave New World*, in which humans are cloned and mass-produced in 'Hatcheries' (it was Haldane who later gave us the word 'clone'). Fast-forward almost a century, and scientists have now trialled ectogenesis on sheep and are exploring its potential for saving dangerously premature babies.

Haldane took no prisoners as he hurtled through the ages and all the major sciences, weighing up what was still to be done. Perhaps because it was his discipline, he was convinced that the next exciting scientific discoveries would be made not in physics but in biology. So, his Daedalus is not the familiar pioneer of flight but the first genetic engineer – the designer of the contraption that enabled King Minos's wife to mate with a bull and produce the Minotaur. Predictions have an unstable afterlife; their truth changes with the world, and while Haldane was brilliant on – and made a major contribution to – genetics, he was sceptical about the possibility of nuclear power. In the wake of the Second World War, and the realities of atom bombs, hydrogen bombs and nuclear power stations, his view of the sciences appeared wide of the mark. Later, when the Human Genome Project became news, he emerged as a prophet again. But while biotech certainly still preoccupies us two decades on, it is the computer that we see ushering in the definitive transformations of the age: artificial intelligence, machine learning, blockchain. And, remarkably, the computer is the one major modern development that not only Haldane but all the To-Day and To-Morrow writers missed.

By 1931, when the series was wound up, it ran to 110 books. They covered many of the subjects that mattered most at the time, from the future of marriage to the future of war, the future of art to the future of the British Empire. Most of To-Day and To-morrow's contributors were progressive, rationalist and intelligent, in favour of a World State and sceptical of eugenics. They wrote well, and were sometimes very funny, and the essays on the future of clothes and the future of nonsense in particular are wonderfully eccentric. And, of course, Haldane wasn't the only visionary. Many of the other writers contributed equally far-sighted ideas: Dora Russell suggested something akin to universal basic income for mothers; J. D. Bernal imagined wirelessly networked cyborgs – a cross between social media and the internet of things; while Vera Brittain waxed confident about the enshrinement of women's rights in law.

What really stands out now is how, on the whole, the authors seemed to feel freer to be imaginative about the future than our contemporaries tend to be when they make predictions. There seems to be something about the long-form essay that freed the To-Day and To-morrow authors to see further ahead than a short journalistic piece could. Pursuing the logic of an individual vision, while also responding to what others projected, led them to dive deep into their topics in ways that are hard for the more tightly collaborative think-tank approaches of today to replicate. They were also more constructive than most of our contemporary future-thinkers. Of course we'd be mad not to worry about the climate crisis, the mass displacement of people(s), the risks of AI, new diseases (I'm writing this at the height – *maybe* – of COVID-19), asteroid collision and other apocalyptic scenarios. But if we're not only to survive these but also to thrive, we need to think beyond them as well as about them.

We are now almost a century on from the launch of To-Day and Tomorrow, and it feels like the right time to try this thought experiment again. So, for this first set of FUTURES, we have assembled a diverse group of brilliant writers with provocative ideas and visions. The point is not so much to prophesy as to generate new ideas about possibilities that could help us realise a future we might want to inhabit. To-Day and To-Morrow launched visions that helped create the modern world. The challenges we face now are, obviously, different from those of the 1920s and 30s. But our aspirations for FUTURES are the same. We want to change the conversation about what lies ahead so we can better imagine, understand and articulate the new worlds we might want to create.

Professor Max Saunders, March 2020

Max Saunders's Imagined Futures: Writing, Science, and Modernity in the To-Day and To-Morrow Book Series, 1923–31 *was published by Oxford University Press in 2019.*

FURTHER READING

Aiken, Mary, *The Cyber Effect: A Pioneering Cyberpsychologist Explains How Human Behaviour Changes Online*, John Murray Press, London, 2016

Alter, Adam, *Irresistible: The Rise of Addictive Technology and the Business of Keeping Us Hooked*, Penguin Publishing Group, New York, 2017

Ansari, Aziz with Klinenberg, Eric, *Modern Romance*, Penguin Press, New York, 2015

Bates, Laura, *Men Who Hate Women: From Incels to Pickup Artists: The Truth About Extreme Misogyny and How it Affects Us All*, Simon & Schuster, London, 2020

Buss, David M., *The Evolution of Desire: Strategies of Human Mating*, Basic Books, New York, 2016

Carr, Nicholas, *The Shallows: What the Internet Is Doing to Our Brains*, W. W. Norton & Company, New York, 2010

Carr, Nicholas, *Utopia Is Creepy: And Other Provocations*, W. W. Norton & Company, New York, 2016

Dunbar, Robin, *The Science of Love and Betrayal*, Faber & Faber, London, 2012

Eyal, Nir, *Hooked: How to Build Habit-Forming Products*, Portfolio Penguin, New York, 2014

Fisher, Helen, *Why We Love: The Nature and Chemistry of Romantic Love*, Henry Holt and Co., New York, 2005

Grigoriadis, Vanessa, *Blurred Lines: Rethinking Sex, Power, and Consent on Campus*, Houghton Mifflin Harcourt, New York, 2018

Hodgson, Nichi, *The Curious History of Dating*, Robinson, London, 2017

Knox, Clement, *Strange Antics: A History of Seduction*, William Collins, London, 2020

Kringelbach, Morten L., *The Pleasure Center: Trust Your Animal Instincts*, Oxford University Press, New York, 2009

Levy, Ariel, *Female Chauvinist Pigs: Women and the Rise of Raunch Culture*, Pocket Books, London, 2005

Nelson, Maggie, *The Argonauts*, Graywolf Press, Minneapolis, 2015

Orenstein, Peggy, *Boys & Sex: Young Men on Hookups, Love, Porn, Consent, and Navigating the New Masculinity*, Harper, New York, 2020

Orenstein, Peggy, *Cinderella Ate My Daughter: Dispatches From the Front Lines of the New Girlie-Girl Culture*, Harper, New York, 2011

Perel, Esther, *Mating in Captivity: Unlocking Erotic Intelligence*, HarperCollins, New York, 2006

Rudder, Christian, *Dataclysm: Who We Are (When We Think No One's Looking)*, 4th Estate, London, 2014

Schwartz, Barry, *The Paradox of Choice: Why More is Less*, HarperCollins, New York, 2004

Slater, Dan, *Love in the Time of Algorithms*, Current, New York, 2013

Strimpel, Zoe, *Seeking Love in Modern Britain: Gender, Dating and the Rise of 'the Single'*, Bloomsbury Academic, London, 2020

Turkle, Sherry, *Alone Together: Why We Expect More from Technology and Less from Each Other*, Basic Books, New York, 2011

Turkle, Sherry, *Reclaiming Conversation: The Power of Talk in a Digital Age*, Penguin Publishing Group, New York, 2015

Weigel, Moira, *Labor of Love: The Invention of Dating*, Farrar, Straus and Giroux, New York, 2016

Witt, Emily, *Future Sex: A New Kind of Free Love*, Farrar, Straus and Giroux, New York, 2016

ACKNOWLEDGEMENTS

With my deepest, heartfelt gratitude to:

The friends & early angels who championed my writing

The editors who have given me a platform to share it

My interviewees, for fielding the grilling

Lisa Gee & Matt d'Ancona

Elizabeth Sheinkman & Kate Evans at PFD

DeAndra Lupu, Amy Winchester & John Mitchinson at Unbound

My son, Max, for the boundless, unbridled joy

My parents, Maria & Anany Levitin, for the opportunities that allowed me to find my voice

And to Lisa Marino & Michael Uriely, whose outsized impact in their too-short lives spurred an attempt to forge something lasting from what James Salter called 'the great heap of days'.

NOTES

1   Mandy Len Catron, 'To fall in love with anyone, do this', *New York Times*, 9 January 2015, available at www.nytimes.com/2015/01/11/style/modern-love-to-fall-in-love-with-anyone-do-this.html

2   Michael Rosenfeld, Reuben J. Thomas and Sonia Hausen, 'Disintermediating your friends: how online dating in the United States displaces other ways of meeting', *Proceedings of the National Academy of Sciences*, 116, 36, 2019, available at web.stanford.edu/~mrosenfe/Rosenfeld_et_al_Disintermediating_Friends.pdf

3   Eir Nolsoe, 'How do Brits find love?', YouGov, 13 February 2020, available at yougov.co.uk/topics/relationships/articles-reports/2020/02/13/how-do-brits-find-love

4   eharmony, 'Over 50% of couples will meet online by 2031', available at www.eharmony.co.uk/dating-advice/online-dating-unplugged/over-50-of-couples-will-meet-online-by-2031#.XF-EAc9KhTZ

5   Gareth Tyson, Vasile C. Perta, et al., 'A first look at user activity on Tinder', ResearchGate, July 2016, available at www.researchgate.net/publication/305007166_A_First_Look_at_User_Activity_on_Tinder

6   Nick Bilton, 'Tinder, the fast-growing dating app, taps an age-old truth', *New York Times*, 30 October 2014, available at www.nytimes.com/2014/10/30/fashion/tinder-the-fast-growing-dating-app-taps-an-age-old-truth.html

7   Jean M. Twenge, Ryne A. Sherman and Brooke E. Wells, 'Sexual inactivity during young adulthood is more common among U.S. millennials and iGen', PubMed, February 2017, available at pubmed.ncbi.nlm.nih.gov/27480753

8   Trong Viggo Grøntvedt, Mons Bendixen, et al., 'Hook, line and sinker: do Tinder matches and meet ups lead to one-night stands?', *Evolutionary Psychological Science*, 5, pp. 109–118, 2020, available at link.springer.com/article/10.1007/s40806-019-00222-z

9   Dan Slater, *Love in the Time of Algorithms*, Penguin Group, USA, 2013, p. 63.

10 eharmony, 'Scientists reveal the most attractive words to use on your profile', available at www.eharmony.co.uk/dating-advice/online-dating-unplugged/scientists-reveal-the-most-attractive-words-to-use-on-your-profile

11 Lindsay Dodgson, 'Using these words in your dating profile will get you the most matches, according to dating app Badoo', Insider, 30 August 2018, available at www.insider.com/words-to-put-in-your-dating-profile-to-get-most-matches-2018-8

12 Christian Rudder, *Dataclysm: Who We Are*, 4th Estate, London, 2016, p. 6.

13 Douglas T. Kenrick and Sara E. Gutierres, 'Contrast effects and judgments of physical attractiveness when beauty becomes a

social problem', *Journal of Personality and Social Psychology*, 38, 1, 1980, pp. 131–40, available at www.beauty-review.nl/wp-content/uploads/2014/06/Contrast-effects-and-judgments-of-physical-attractiveness-When-beauty-becomes-a-social-problem.pdf

14 Elizabeth E. Bruch and M. E. J. Newman, 'Aspirational pursuit of mates in online dating markets', *Science Advances*, 4, 8, 2018, available at advances.sciencemag.org/content/4/8/eaap9815?-mod=article_inline

15 Jonathan D. D'Angelo and Cataline L. Toma, 'There are plenty of fish in the sea', *Media Psychology*, 20, 1, 2017, available at www.tandfonline.com/doi/abs/10.1080/15213269.2015.1121827

16 Daniel T. Gilbert and Jane E. J. Ebert, 'Decisions and revisions: the affective forecasting of changeable outcomes', *Journal of Personality and Social Psychology*, 82, 4, 2002, pp. 503–14, available at www.danielgilbert.com/Gilber%20t&%20Ebert%20(DECISIONS %20&%20REVISIONS).pdf

17 Eli J. Finkel and Paul W. Eastwick, 'Speed-dating', *Current Directions in Psychological Science*, 2008, available at journals.sagepub.com/doi/10.1111/j.1467-8721.2008.00573.x

18 Anna Brown, 'Lesbian, gay and bisexual online daters report positive experiences – but also harassment', Pew Research Center, 9 April 2020, available at www.pewresearch.org/fact-tank/2020/04/09/lesbian-gay-and-bisexual-online-daters-report-positive-experiences-but-also-harassment

19 Michael Rosenfeld, 'How Tinder and the dating apps are and are not changing dating and mating in the U.S.', in *Families and Technology*, edited by Jennifer Van Hook, Susan M. McHale and Valarie King, Springer, 2017, available at web.stanford.edu/~mrosenfe/Rosenfeld_Tinder_and_dating_apps.pdf

20 Monica Anderson, Emily A. Vogels and Erica Turner, 'The virtues and downsides of online dating', Pew Research Center, 6 February 2020, available at www.pewresearch.org/internet/2020/02/06/the-virtues-and-downsides-of-online-dating

21 John M. Grohol, 'Study questions whether women are more selective at dating', Live Science, 29 September 2009, available at www.livescience.com/7918-study-questions-women-selective-dating.html

22 Mike Brown, 'Is Tinder a match for millennials?', LendEDU, 22 March 2017, available at lendedu.com/blog/tinder-match-millennials

23 David M. Buss, *The Evolution of Desire: Strategies of Human Mating*, Basic Books, New York, 2016.

24 Alex Williams, 'The End of Courtship?', *New York Times*, 13 January 2013, available at www.nytimes.com/2013/01/13/fashion/the-end-of-courtship.html

25 Singles in America, 2019 survey, available at www.singlesinamerica.com

26 Angela J. Jacques-Tiura, Antonia Abbey, et al., 'Why do some men misperceive women's sexual intentions more frequently than others do? An application of the confluence model',

Personality and Social Psychology Bulletin, 33, 11, 2007, pp. 1467–80, available at www.ncbi.nlm.nih.gov/pmc/articles/PMC4484569/ #:~:text=Men%20who%20drink%20alcohol%20in,alcohol's%20 psychological%20and%20pharmacological%20effects

27 Joseph E. Padgett and Lisa Wade, 'Hookup culture and higher education', in *Handbook of Contemporary Feminism*, Taylor & Francis, 2018, available at www.researchgate.net/publication/319988180_ Hookup_Culture_and_Higher_Education

28 Elizabeth A. Armstrong, Paula England and Alison C. K. Fogarty, 'Accounting for women's orgasm and sexual enjoyment in college hook-ups and relationships', *American Sociological Review*, 2012, available at journals.sagepub.com/doi/ full/10.1177/0003122412445802

29 David A. Frederick, H. Kate St. John, et al., 'Differences in orgasm frequency among gay, lesbian, bisexual, and heterosexual men and women in a U.S. national sample', *Archives of Sexual Behavior*, 47, 2018, pp. 273–88, available at link.springer.com/ article/10.1007/s10508-017-0939-z?wt_mc=Affiliate.Commis- sionJunction.3.EPR1089.DeepLink

30 Victoria Waldersee, 'Half of Brits don't know where the vagina is – and it's not just the men', YouGov, 8 March 2019, available at yougov.co.uk/topics/health/articles-reports/2019/03/08/half- brits-dont-know-where-vagina-and-its-not-just

31 Amy Fleming, 'Is porn making young men impotent?', *Guardian*, 11 March 2019, available at www.theguardian.com/lifeandstyle/2019/ mar/11/young-men-porn-induced-erectile-dysfunction

32 Cicely Alice Marston and Ruth Lewis, 'Anal heterosex among young people and implications for health promotion: a qualitative study in the UK', *BMJ*, 4, 8, 2014, available at www.research-gate.net/publication/264744796_Anal_heterosex_among_young_people_and_implications_for_health_promotion_A_qualitative_study_in_the_UK

33 Ellen Scott, 'These are the words you should never use on your online dating profiles', *Metro*, 17 June 2016, available at metro.co.uk/2016/06/17/these-are-the-words-you-should-never-use-on-your-online-dating-profiles-5950323

34 The Dating Apocalypse, available at thedatingapocalypse.com

35 OkCupid, 'The big lies people tell in online dating', OkCupid, 7 July 2010, available at theblog.okcupid.com/the-big-lies-people-tell-in-online-dating-a9e3990d6ae2

36 Nick Bilton, 'Tinder, the fastest-growing dating app, taps an age-old truth'

37 Dan Ariely, Talks at Google: 'On Dating & Relationships', 11 November 2015, available at www.youtube.com/watch?v=RS8R2TKrYio

38 Michael Rosenfeld, 'How Tinder and the dating apps are and are not changing dating and mating in the U.S.'

39 Annie Lord, 'Do millennial men just like having the option of sex – then flaking at the last minute?', *Vogue*, 17 July 2020, available at www.vogue.co.uk/arts-and-lifestyle/article/sexual-rejection

40 Monica Anderson, Emily A. Vogels and Erica Turner, 'The virtues and downsides of online dating'.

41 Jonathan Franzen, 'Liking is for cowards. Go for what hurts', *New York Times*, 28 May 2011, available at www.nytimes.com/2011/05/29/opinion/29franzen.html

42 Laura Hilgers, 'The ridiculous fantasy of a "no drama" relationship', *New York Times*, 20 July 2019, available at www.nytimes.com/2019/07/20/opinion/sunday/tinder-bumble-okcupid-drama.html

43 Stephanie Coontz, 'How to make your marriage gayer', *New York Times*, 13 February 2020, available at www.nytimes.com/2020/02/13/opinion/sunday/marriage-housework-gender-happiness.html

44 Delvv, 'Delvv digital habits 2016 survey findings', available at delvv.com/downloads/survey_2016_results.pdf

45 Chelsea Ritschel, 'Sexting can negatively impact a relationship, researchers found', *Independent*, 31 January 2018, available at www.independent.co.uk/life-style/sexting-relationship-insecure-technology-communication-research-a8188031.html and Helen Metella, 'Lots of sexting can wreck a romance', Phys.org, 30 January 2018, available at phys.org/news/2018-01-lots-sexting-romance.html

46 'National crime agency reports increase in recorded rapes related to online dating', Rape Crisis, 6 February 2016, available at rapecrisis.org.uk/news/latest-news/national-crime-agency-reports-increase-in-recorded-rapes-related-to-online-dating

47 Ibid.

48 OkCupid, 'Feminism in dating: it's not about making the first move, but having the choice', OkCupid, 8 December 2017, avail-

able at theblog.okcupid.com/feminism-in-dating-its-not-about-making-the-first-move-but-having-the-choice-f4f2891dd4c9

49 Matthew Smith, 'Sexual harassment: how the genders and generations see the issue differently', YouGov, 1 November 2017, available at yougov.co.uk/topics/lifestyle/articles-reports/2017/11/01/sexual-harassment-how-genders-and-generations-see-

50 Maia Szalavitz, 'Shocker: empathy dropped 40% in college students since 2000', *Psychology Today*, 28 May 2010, available at www.psychologytoday.com/blog/born-love/201005/shocker-empathy-dropped-40-in-college-students-2000

51 Sherry Turkle, *Reclaiming Conversation: The Power of Talk in a Digital Age*, Penguin Publishing Group, New York, 2015, p. 11.

52 'Digital content provider "Confi" unveils innovative study on college sexual assault', Confi, 21 November 2016, available at confi.co/research-press-release-2016

53 Peggy Orenstein, 'It's not that men don't know what consent is', *New York Times*, 23 February 2019, available at www.nytimes.com/2019/02/23/opinion/sunday/sexual-consent-college.html

54 GQ freelance political writer, 'Neil Strauss' new book is complete and utter bollocks', *GQ*, 5 November 2015, available at www.gq-magazine.co.uk/article/neil-strauss-the-game-the-truth-bollocks

55 Dougal Shaw, 'Coronavirus: Tinder boss says "dramatic" changes to dating', BBC News, 21 May 2020, available at www.bbc.co.uk/news/business-52743454

56 'Q1 2020 – Letter to shareholders', Match Group, 5 May 2020, available at https://s22.q4cdn.com/279430125/files/doc_financials/2020/q1/Match-Group-Q1-2020-Shareholder-Letter-(1).pdf

57 OkCupid, 'Love in the time of corona: massive spikes in matching, messaging and virtual dates around the world', OkCupid, 4 April 2020, available at theblog.okcupid.com/love-in-the-time-of-corona-massive-spikes-in-matching-messaging-and-virtual-dates-around-the-ec12c49eab86

58 Dougal Shaw, 'Coronavirus: Tinder boss says "dramatic" changes to dating'.

59 MacKenzie Sigalos, 'Why the coronavirus might change dating forever', CNBC, 25 May 2020, available at www.cnbc.com/2020/05/25/why-the-coronavirus-might-change-dating-forever.html

60 Kate Lloyd, 'Dating apps have changed during lockdown, but is it for the better?', *Time Out*, 7 April 2020, available at www.timeout.com/london/news/dating-apps-have-changed-during-lockdown-but-is-it-for-the-better-040720

61 'Investor relations', Match Group, available at ir.mtch.com/overview/default.aspx

62 Steven Bertoni, 'Tinder hits $3 billion valuation after Match Group converts options', *Forbes*, 31 August 2017, available at www.forbes.com/sites/stevenbertoni/2017/08/31/tinder-hits-3-billion-valuation-after-match-group-converts-options/#acfad0334f9b

63   Business Overview, Match Group, February 2020, available at s22.q4cdn.com/279430125/files/doc_downloads/2020/02/Match-Group-Business-Overview-February-2020-vFFF.pdf

64   Fremantle, Liz (@LizFremantle). 'The end of an era! @guardian Soulmates is shutting up shop. Where now will I find perfectly nice people I don't fancy to have a drink with and then never see again? #dating.' 14 May 2020, 9:56 am. Tweet.

65   Zoe Strimpel, 'Singles are worse off without Guardian Soulmates', *Spectator Life*, 16 May 2020, available at life.spectator.co.uk/articles/singles-are-worse-off-without-guardian-soulmates

66   Jennifer Boeder, 'Would you rather meet your significant other IRL or through a dating app?', Tylt, 9 July 2018, available at thetylt.com/culture/meet-irl-or-online

67   Dr Alexandra Solomon, 'The Marriage 101 course at Northwestern University', available at www.dralexandrasolomon.com/marriage-101-course

68   Michael Rosenfeld, Reuben J. Thomas and Sonia Hausen, 'Disintermediating your friends: how online dating in the United States displaces other ways of meeting'.

69   'Automating Tinder with artificial intelligence', Crockpot Veggies, available at www.crockpotveggies.com/2016/07/26/automate-tinder-artificial-intelligence.html

70   Ethan Czuy Levine, Debby Herbenick, et al., 'Open relationships, non-consensual nonmonogamy, and monogamy among U.S. adults: findings from the 2012 national survey of sexual health and

behaviour', *Archives of Sexual Behavior*, 47, 5, 2018, pp. 1439–50, available at www.ncbi.nlm.nih.gov/pmc/articles/PMC5958351

71 Dan Savage, '3 Things We Get Wrong About Love', 2 October 2017, available at www.youtube.com/watch?v=brZIb4MG80A

72 Peggy Orenstein, *Boys & Sex: Young Men on Hookups, Love, Porn, Consent, and Navigating the New Masculinity*, Harper, New York, 2020, p. 121.

73 Debby Hebernick, Vanessa Schick, et al., 'Pain experienced during vaginal and anal intercourse with our-sex partners: findings from a nationally representative probability study in the United States', *The Journal of Sexual Medicine*, 4, 2015, pp. 1040–51, available at pubmed.ncbi.nlm.nih.gov/25648245

74 Lili Loofbourow, 'The female price of male pleasure', *The Week*, 25 January 2018, available at theweek.com/articles/749978/female-price-male-pleasure

75 Peggy Orenstein, 'It's not that men don't know what consent is'.

76 Singles in America, available at www.singlesinamerica.com

77 Chantelle Otten, 'Your 2020 resolution? Make the first move on Bumble', The Beehive, 10 January 2020, available at thebeehive. bumble.com/au-blog/2020bumbleresolution#:~:text=On%20 Bumble%2C%20when%20it%20comes,then%20leads%20 to%20a%20date.&text=Start%20small%2C%20whether% 20on%20Bumble,a%20deep%2C%20meaningful%20conversa-tion%20topic.

78 Singles in America, available at www.singlesinamerica.com

79 Esther Perel, *Mating in Captivity: Unlocking Erotic Intelligence*, HarperCollins, New York, 2006, pp. 95–96.

80 'Swipe left: dating apps have killed romance', Intelligence[2] Debates, available at www.intelligencesquaredus.org/debates/swipe-left-dating-apps-have-killed-romance

Unbound is the world's first crowdfunding publisher, established in 2011.

We believe that wonderful things can happen when you clear a path for people who share a passion. That's why we've built a platform that brings together readers and authors to crowdfund books they believe in – and give fresh ideas that don't fit the traditional mould the chance they deserve.

This book is in your hands because readers made it possible. Everyone who pledged their support is listed below. Join them by visiting unbound.com and supporting a book today.

With special thanks to Jo Greenslade and Ark Schools

Caspar Addyman
Kathy Allen
John Attridge
William Ayles
Stuart Banks
David Barker
Stephen Beagrie
Ghassan Bejjani
Sarah Bennett
James Benussi

Steve Bindley
Kate Bird
Ian Blatchford
Su Bonfanti
Ed Bonnell
Stuart Bowdler
John Boxall
Zara Bredin
Catherine Breslin
Fabia Bromovsky

Victoria Bryant
Nicki Burns
Paul David Burns
Imogen Butler
Steve Byrne
Bob Callard
Ella Cape-Davenhill
NJ Cesar
Neil Chavner
Brendan Clarke

Nick Clarke

Peter Clasen

Jane Clifford

Fiona Clifft

Rhonda Cole

David-John Collins

Robert Collins

Alexander Colmer

Laura Colombino

Joseph Cordery

Andrew Correia

Peter Cosgrove

Nicola Crowell

Paolo Cuomo

Mary Curnock
    Cook

Matthew d'Ancona

Tom Daly

Eileen Davidson

Joshua Davies

Edmund Davison

Victoria Davison

Sarah Denton

Jeremy Dicker

Lewis Dimmick

Kevin Donnellon

Linda Edge

Helen Edwards

Michael Elliott

Dominic Emery

Nic Fallows

Joanna Flood

Graham Folmer

Cedric Fontanille

Robert Forsyth

Oliver Francis

D Franklin

The FUTURES
    team

Josh Gaillemin

Brian Gee

Lisa Gee

Sarah Gee

Charley Gilbert

Tom Gillingwater

Jordan Goble

George Goodfellow

John Gordon

Molly Gordon

Paul Gould

Brice Goureau

Melanie Gow

Keith Grady

Marlies Gration

Jon Gray

Scott Greenwell

Georgia Greer

John Grout

Steve Grycuk

Nicola Haggett

Greg Halfacre

Elizabeth Hall

Skye Hallam

Chloe Hardy

Nicola Harford

Richard Harvey

Nick Helweg-
    Larsen

Paul Higgins

Gemma Hitchens

Maggie Hobbs

Meaghan Hook

Simon Howard

Nick Hubble

Simon Huggins

Jenny Hynd

Maggie Jack

Andy Johnson

Rebecca Jones

Danny Josephs

Tanu Kaskinen

Matthew Keegan

Christopher Kelly

Hilary Kemp

Luke Kemp

Fraser Kerr

Adam Khan

Dan Kieran

Andrew Knight

Christine Knight-
    Maunder

Lauren Knussen

Florian Kogler

Michael Kowalski

Simon Krystman

Nikki Land

Ben Lappin

Lyndsey Lawrence

Benedict Leigh

Fiona Lensvelt

Max Lensvelt

Sonny Leong

Miriam Levitin

Joanne Limburg

Linds

Valerie Lindsay

Ivan Lowe

Brian Lunn

Nicola Lynch

Rob MacAndrew

Andrew MacGarvey

Jem Mackay

Innes Macleod

Lewis MacRae

Paul Martin

Chris Matthias

Jenny McCullough

Michael McDowall

John McGowan

Neil McLaren

Adrian Melrose

John Mitchinson

Ronald Mitchinson

Kyna Morgan

Ian Morley

Tony Mulvahil

Robin Mulvihill

Peter Mummery

Tessa Murray

Janet Musgrove

James Nash

Carlo Navato

Kelvin Nel

John New

Sorcha Ní
    Mhaonaigh

Christopher Norris

Tim O'Connor

Mark O'Neill

Brian Padley

Michael Paley

Euan Palmer

Nic Parsons

Jaynesh Patel

Don Paterson

Sumit Paul-
    Choudhury

Matthew Pearson

Pauline Peirce

Nick Petre

Benjamin Poliak

Justin Pollard

Harriet Posner

Samantha Potter

Mark Poulson

Kate Pullinger

Slam Raman

Padraig Reade

Colette Reap

Suzanne Reynolds

John Rice Doyle

Stephen Ross

Charlotte Rump

Stuart Rutherford

Keith Ruttle

Cassedy Ryan

Ruth Sacks

Luke Sanders

Martin Saugnac

Max Saunders

Eleanor Scharer

Daniel Schwickerath

Duncan Scovil

Alexander Sehmer

Rossa Shanks

Gillian Shearn

Paul Skinner

Christopher Smith

Jan Smith

Katie Smith

Matthew Spicer

Paul Squires

Wendy Staden

Nicola Stanhope

Keith Stewart

Freddie Stockler

Nick Stringer

Elizabeth Suffling

Gilane Tawadros

Georgette Taylor

Richard Taylor

Bronwen Thomas

Luke Thornton

Lydia Titterington

Sophie Truepenny

Mark Turner

Geoff Underwood

Maarten van den
Belt

Suzan Vanneck

Danielle Vides

Emma Visick

Gabriel Vogt

Claire Walker

Sir Harold Walker

Suzi Watford

Richard White

John Williams

Ross Williams

Catherine
Williamson

Philip Wilson

Luke Young

Angelique &
Stefano Zuppet